First published in Great Britain

2023 by Jack Soley

This publication is the second edition published in 2025.

Copyright © Jack Soley, 2023

Jack Soley has asserted his moral right to be identified as the Author of this work in accordance with the Copyright Designs and Patents Act 1988.

All rights reserved. No part of this publication may be reproduced, stored in a retrieval system, or transmitted in any form or by any means, electronic, mechanical, photocopying, recording or otherwise, without the prior permission of the publisher.

A catalogue record for this book is available from the British Library.

All opinions are those of the author and do not represent the views of the publishing company or their affiliates.

This book is published by Pomerak Ventures Ltd, registered in England & Wales under the company number 15578139.

ISBN: 9781917706032

Foreword

Well… the last book was such a good adventure when it was released in January 2023; after then, I knew I wanted to write the sequel, given how successful I felt it was, and here I am.

I must thank everyone who left their comments about my book online the first time around, my friends and family, who were there to support me, and everyone who went out of their way to buy a copy, whether it was the paperback or the electronic version. I think the most prominent achievement was in one of the categories on Amazon at a point in early February; the book was the 2nd hottest new release and the 11th best-selling in the "Amazing Facts" category; since that time, the book had to be re-written and a second edition published due to spelling mistakes which quite honestly I should have picked up the first time round.

Anyway, here's a second helping of some useless facts and knowledge you or your friends didn't ask for. You can purchase my other books from Amazon.com in both paperback & e-book format including the prequel to this work. As always, thank you for your continued support.

Another 500 Useless Facts That Nobody Wanted To Know

1. Derived from "dead horse", the name of the fear of tomato ketchup is called "Mortuusequusphobia".

2. Roughly 10% of Scotland's land is used for grouse shooting.

3. The term "fish finger" was first referenced in the Tamworth Herald in 1900.

4. The first track of Étienne De Crecy's 1996 album "Super Discount" has a run time of 10 minutes and 6 seconds.

5. Ice cubes made from ordinary water is not subject to VAT in the UK.

6. A study in 2018 reported that more than half of parents with more than one child, preferred the youngest.

7. The most ordered cocktail in the world, is the Margarita.

8. The A249 is a major road running from Maidstone to Sheerness in South East England, it has a total length of 18.6 miles or 29.9 kilometres.

9. Until March 2023, Denmark used to follow Mean Solar Time which meant the country would ignore Coordinated Universal Time and as a result, its clocks would be ahead or behind a few milliseconds throughout the year.

10. Coordinated Universal Time is also known by its other name "UTC", English speakers wanted it to be known as "CUT" and French speakers wanted it to be known as "TUC", but a compromise was made as the initials wanted to be the same around the world.

11. In 1923, jockey Frank Hayes won a horse race at Belmont Park despite suffering a heart attack; this makes Hayes the

first and only known jockey to have won a race after death.

12. Harland Sanders, the founder of the KFC franchise was made an honourary colonel of Kentucky by the governor of the state in 1935, Ruby Laffoon.

13. During the opening ceremony of the 2012 Olympic Games in London, the corgis that appeared with the Queen and Daniel Craig were called Willow, Holly, and Monty.

14. When the arcade game "Space Invaders" was released in Japan in 1978, so many punters journeyed to arcades, a nationwide coin shortage followed.

15. James Bond actor Daniel Craig's middle name is Wroughton.

16. The village of Wroughton in Wiltshire, England was home to RAF Wroughton which closed in the 1990s; part of the site has been used as a racing track in The Grand Tour series.

17. Richard Hammond's first motorcycle was a Honda MTX50.

18. As of April 2022, only 15 U.S. states including Washington D.C. don't require ID in order to vote.

19. Before it changed to John Lennon Airport in 2001, Liverpool's International Airport was originally called Speke Airport.

20. David Bowie's 1976 album "Station to Station" was recorded at Cherokee Studios in Los Angeles and The Record Plant in New York City.

21. A drone bee's sole purpose is to mate, after mating the abdomen rips open and the drone will most likely die, but if the male survives, the bee is kicked out of the hive to die alone.

22. The Shatabdi Express are a series of high speed passenger trains operated by Indian Railways, they were first introduced on the 14th November 1988 to

mark the birth centenary of India's first prime minister Jawaharal Nehru.

23. Prayagraj in Uttar Pradesh, India has an elevation of 98 metres above sea level.

24. The Hindi language is an official language in India and is a recognised minority language in South Africa and the United Arab Emirates.

25. In 2013, only 15% of the population of the United Arab Emirates were full citizens of the country.

26. British Airways' only flights to Hamad International Airport in Doha, Qatar are from London Gatwick with seasonal flights from London Heathrow.

27. "Konkors Kanzunetta Indipendenza" is a song competition held every year near September 21st in Malta to mark the country's independence day, the winner of the competition in 2013 was Fabrizio Faniello.

28. In the Eurovision Song Contest, there is an annual exchange where Cyprus and Greece almost always award each other 12 points; In 2015, both countries awarded 12 points to Italy.

29. In 1997, snooker player Ronnie O'Sullivan achieved the world record for the fastest 147 break, setting it in 5 minutes and 8 seconds.

30. English snooker player Kyren Wilson, earned a gold medal at the 2017 World Games.

31. In 1992, Continental Cablevision started a sting operation to catch cable thieves by displaying a phone number during a pay-per-view boxing match where customers could claim a free T-shirt, the number would only be visible to viewers with illegal equipment and therefore the authorities would also be informed of these cable pirates.

32. In a 2018 report, the most popular sandwiches in the UK of the 2010s decade are Hummus and falafel, BBQ pulled pork, avocado, chicken and avocado, and brie and grape.

33. In 2022, a study discovered that Americans prefer boiled eggs over any other serving method.

34. The Easter Egg came around because during Lent, when Christians fasted; eggs were one of the forbidden foods to eat so when Easter Sunday arrived, eating eggs was long awaited.

35. The largest 5 exporters of Chocolate in 2021, in descending order are Germany, Belgium, Italy, Poland, and the Netherlands.

36. The largest 5 exporters of Cocoa beans in 2021, in descending order are Cote D'Ivoire, Ghana, Ecuador, Nigeria, and Cameroon.

37. Lagos, Nigeria has a population of over 24 million people and was the national

capital of Nigeria until 12th December 1991.

38. The Men's FIH Hockey Junior World Cup was awarded to Argentina in 2021 and the country with the most titles is Germany with 6 titles.

39. The song "Jerk It Out" by the Swedish band Caesars has appeared in commercials for the iPod Shuffle, Coca-Cola, Nivea, Renault, and multiple video games.

40. On the Sony Playstation 2, there are towers that appear on the startup screen when the system is switched on, a new tower is added for each game you've played on the console and the height of the tower indicates how long the games have been played.

41. Guy and Howard Lawrence are the brothers that form the electronic & house duo Disclosure, they have been nominated for 7 Grammy Awards but as of 2023, not won a single one.

42. According to a 2021 survey, the sexiest hair colour is blonde.

43. The most common eye colour in Turkey, is green.

44. Male mosquitoes have bushier antennae than female mosquitoes.

45. Johann Wilhelm Meigen was a German entomologist famous for his work on Flies.

46. The first animals deliberately sent into space were fruit flies aboard a U.S.-launched V-2 rocket on 20 February 1947.

47. In the 2022-23 Football League Two season, Gillingham F.C. finished in 17th place with 55 points.

48. Rochester was recognised as a City from 1211 to 1998, the city status was taken away due to an administrative error where a clerk had mistakenly forgot to submit paperwork and the only

way for the city to be reinstated is for the monarch to declare it a city.

49. At 349ft, the Capitol Center is the tallest building in South Carolina.

50. The current flag of Rwanda was adopted on the 25th October 2001.

51. Stuffed Crust Pizza was first invented by Patty Scheibmeir in 1995.

52. In 1892, Robert Sputh invented the drinks coaster.

53. The official word for someone who loves cheese is a turophile.

54. The most hated word in the English language is "Moist".

55. The second most hated word in the English language is "Flap".

56. At the time of the 2011 census, Havant in Hampshire had a population of 45,826.

57. The survival rate for testicular cancer in the U.S. is 95%.

58. Stinson Hunter was born in Nuneaton.

59. 24 cubed is 13,824.

60. The largest prime number known was discovered in 2018 has 24,862,048 digits.

61. Beatrix's bat was discovered in 1901 by British zoologist Oldfield Thomas.

62. Lieutenant Colonel Wisnu Airfield on the island of Bali, Indonesia has the IATA code WSN.

63. In New Zealand, you are not allowed to name your twin children "Benson and Hedges".

64. Abraham Lincoln expressed his admiration for San Marino in a letter in 1861, saying, "Although your dominion is small, nevertheless your State is one of the most honoured throughout history". In response, they granted him honourary citizenship.

65. Almonds originated in Iran.

66. The real name of the rapper Kool Keith is Keith Matthew Thornton.

67. People often feel the need to pee when there's between 200ml and 350ml of urine in their bladder.

68. Corticotropin is a hormone made in the pituitary gland.

69. According to the original 1891 patent for the toilet paper holder, the toilet paper goes over the top.

70. The collections of the German entomologist August Assmann are now on display at the Museum of Natural History at the University of Wrocław.

71. Bitcoin has been declared as a form of legal currency in El Salvador and the Central African Republic.

72. Around 90% of the land area of Mauritius is sugar cane fields.

73. In Mauritius, 48% of citizens identify as Hindu.

74. Women hiccup less than men.

75. The first musical road is the Asphaltophone, created in 1995 and is based in Gylling, Denmark.

76. As of March 2023, motorcycles up to 50cc do not require at least 1mm of tyre tread in order to pass its annual inspection in the UK, they just need to have a visible tread.

77. The 4th largest producer of corn, is Argentina at 51 million metric tons.

78. Mobile phones sold in Japan must by law have a camera shutter sound on when photos are taken, this is because of privacy concerns.

79. Funai of Japan was the last known company to manufacture VHS equipment, they ceased production in 2016.

80. The first official purchase of the Euro currency was one kilo of lychees on the

French island of Reunion on the 1ˢᵗ January 2002.

81. In the Overwatch video game series, the character Symmetra is Indian, female, an architect, and autistic; she was one of the 21 heroes included in the game's release in 2016.

82. According to Google's Ngram viewer, 2004 was the year when more people wrote about David Bowie than Mick Jagger.

83. The United Kingdom does not have an embassy in the Republic of Comoros but the Comoros is represented by the British Embassy in Madagascar.

84. When Queen Elizabeth II died, it was the first state funeral held in the UK since 1965 after Winston Churchill died.

85. "Are you aching for the blade? That's okay we're insured." are the opening words to the 2001 James song "Getting Away With It (All Messed Up)".

86. The volcanic island of Surtsey in the Vestmannaeyjar of Iceland was jokingly claimed for France by journalists of Paris Match magazine in 1963, around a month after the island itself was formed by volcanic activity.

87. It's legal to smoke marijuana in North Korea.

88. In March 2023, Lebanon had 2 time zones due to a religious dispute; Lebanon's Muslim prime minister decided to delay the implementation of Daylight Saving Time until the end of Ramadan. But the Maronite Church rejected the idea meaning that different people in the country worked on two separate time zones.

89. In 2003, the National Institute of Standards and Technology, a U.S. agency; developed the most expensive jar of peanut butter where scientists analysed and came up with a standard chemical and ingredient composition for

the foodstuff; the price for one jar as of 2023 is $1,107 for 3x 170g jars which works out to just over $2 per gram.

90. It takes almost 4,000 helium balloons to lift a person who weighs 50 kilograms.

91. Louis Braille invented the Braille tactile system, also known as "night writing" so soldiers could communicate safely during the night.

92. Mara Wilson, the star of the 1996 Matilda movie; was the victim of a death hoax in 2000 with the cause being a broken neck.

93. Halland County in Sweden is situated on the western coast of the country and has an area of 5,454 square kilometres.

94. If Erling Haaland didn't play for Norway's national football team, he would have been eligible to play for England as he was born in the English city of Leeds.

95. Jan Åge Fjørtoft, another Norwegian footballer scored 1 premier league goal for Middlesborough in the 1996-97 season.

96. The 19th amendment to the U.S. constitution granted women the right to vote.

97. For the first time in the country's history, Pope Francis gives women the right to vote at the Synod; a body in the Vatican City that gathers the world's bishops together for meetings, following years of demands by women to have voting rights.

98. Cliff Arnall, the man behind the pseudoscientific equation for the most depressing day of the year, calculated that Friday 21st June was the happiest day of 2013.

99. According to frankbuna.com, the most popular coffee based beverage in 2022 was the Latte.

100. On the same poll, the second most popular coffee based beverage was the Mocha, which is my personal favourite.

101. In 2023, the standard rates of income tax in Italy were from 23% to 43%.

102. In 1962, "Tracy" was the 55th most common baby name for a girl born in the United States.

103. In the data set, "Tracey" was ranked 123rd.

104. A marionette is a puppet controlled from above using wires or strings, the name comes from the French for 'little Mary'.

105. The sunset time in San Juan, Puerto Rico on the 9th May 2023 was 6:49pm local time.

106. In a survey conducted by Dulux, Yellow is the least favourite colour, preferred by only five percent of people.

107. The same survey also discovered that men and women tend to dislike Orange as they grow older.

108. In Denmark, it's legal to burn the Danish flag but it's illegal to burn the flag of another nation.

109. A volcanic eruption in the Antarctic was recorded in the year 566.

110. Twyndyllyngs is the longest word in the English language without any vowels.

111. In the Chinese Zodiac, people who are Tigers should marry Dragons, Horses, and Pigs whereas they should avoid other Tigers, Oxen, Snakes, and Monkeys.

112. The 6th studio album from David Bowie "Aladdin Sane" was his first UK number one album.

113. The space suit was invented by Spanish physicist Emilio Herrera Linares.

114.   The lifespan of a pigeon in the wild, is 6 years.

115.   Bufotoxin is a substance that is obtained from the skin glands of the European toad; it causes changes in heart rate and rhythm.

116.   Uncle Spike's Book Exchange based in Windhoek, Namibia; is on the junction of Tal Street & Garten Street.

117.   A charnel house is a vault or building where human skeletal remains are stored. They are often built near churches for depositing bones that are unearthed while digging graves.

118.   "The Charnel House" is a painting created by Spanish painter Pablo Picasso between 1944 and 1945, it's an oil and charcoal on canvas and is currently housed in the Museum of Modern Art in New York.

119. In the year 1900, the Park Row Building in New York was the city's tallest building.

120. If an apple is roughly 3 inches in diameter, it will contain 0.5 grams of protein.

121. In 2023, Greek tourism authorities were in the process of retrofitting 287 beaches across the country with wheelchair ramps to allow more people access to the beach.

122. An average pen can write around 45,000 words before running out of ink.

123. The Chockalog River flows for 2 miles and runs through the U.S. states of Massachusetts and Rhode Island.

124. "Who Ate All the Pies?" is a football chant sung by fans in the UK; it was said that the chant was directed at William "Fatty" Foulke, he had one international cap for England in 1897.

125. The Emoji Movie had a budget of $50 million and took over $217 million at the box office.

126. Patrick Stewart's first television appearance was a fire officer in a 1967 episode of Coronation Street.

127. Venetian Snares' opening track on "The Chocolate Wheelchair Album" heavily samples the theme from the UK soap opera Coronation Street.

128. The highest scoring word in a game of Scrabble is "Oxyphenbutazone" and can net a maximum of 1,778 points.

129. The most common colour of eyes for cats, is yellow/amber.

130. On the 21st March 2006, Twitter was founded and on that day at 9:33pm, @timroberts tweeted: "setting up my mac mini".

131. The original Mac Mini was launched on the 22nd January 2005, and had an introductory price of $499.

132. The 100 U.S. dollar note features an image of the Independence Hall in which the clock indicates the time as 4:10pm.

133. There is a pump organ museum near the village of Barger-Compascuum in Drenthe, Netherlands.

134. On July 25, 2015; Fabrizio Maturani also known as Martufello was the victim of a car accident in Vetralla, reporting the fracture of the nasal septum and other damages to his head and legs.

135. Wesley Williams, also known as "The One Wheel Wonder," holds the Guinness World Record for riding the tallest unicycle. The unicycle measured 9.71 metres, or 31 feet and 10 inches, which is one metre taller than the previous record.

136. In Switzerland, it is forbidden to drive while wearing flip-flops.

137. Christian Friedrich Ludwig Buschmann was a German musical instrument maker and inventor, often credited with inventing the harmonica and accordion.

138. A stevedore; also called a longshoreman, a docker or a dockworker, is a manual laborer who is involved in loading and unloading ships, trucks, trains or airplanes.

139. Uli Maurer is a German professional ice hockey player who currently plays for SC Riessersee of the Oberliga, the third tier of German Ice Hockey.

140. Ueli Maurer is a Swiss politician who was president of the Swiss Confederation in 2013 & 2019.

141. Leon Spencer was an American jazz organist from Houston, Texas. He recorded for Prestige Records in the 1970s.

142. In a 2022 study by autoblog.com, the 2nd least reliable car maker in the U.S. is Tesla.

143. The average house price in Portugal in 2023 is approximately $256 per square foot.

144. Gingerbread men are modelled on Guy Fawkes.

145. Marcelino Núñez was born on the 1st March 2000.

146. The most common surname in the U.S. state of Georgia is Williams.

147. The most common surname in the Republic of Georgia, is Beridze.

148. As of May 2023, the largest jackpot of the Euromillions lottery won, was just under $246 million.

149. The second o in the Google logo is yellow.

150. As of May 2023, the most watched English language series on Netflix, is the 4th season of Stranger Things.

151. Noah Schnapp is an American actor known for his portrayal of Will Byers in Stranger Things.

152. In 1908, Thomas Sullivan was an American tea and coffee importer who shipped out samples of tea packed in silk pouches. Brewing tea using these bags became very popular among his customers and thus he accidentally invented the tea bag.

153. The third Wednesday of every April is marked in the U.S. as "National Banana Day".

154. The Netherlands contains the highest proportion of left-handed people at over 13%.

155. The most common shoe size for men in the U.S. is 10.5.

156. In shoe sizes, if you are size 10.5 in the U.S.; in Europe you are size 44 if Male and 42.5 if Female.

157. "Idealism" is the debut studio album by German electronic music duo Digitalism; it has a runtime of 51 minutes and 44 seconds.

158. The three most common food allergies are Milk, Peanuts, and Shellfish.

159. As of 2021, Spotify has more than 382 million monthly users among which 172 million are paying subscribers.

160. Athazagoraphobia is a fear of forgetting someone or something, as well as a fear of being forgotten.

161. According to a 2021 survey, the worst quality in a man is being inconsiderate.

162. In the same survey, the 5th worst quality was being a cheater.

163.   1 in 5 British adults admitted to having had an affair. Of those who have had an affair, only half have stopped after having one.

164.   Cadbury was the first company to use heart-shaped boxes in 1861.

165.   The speed limit on major highways in the Gambia is 70kph.

166.   An article from the Daily Mirror in 2017 reported that the ideal age that a child should know how to tie their shoelaces is eight.

167.   According to careerprofiles.info, in 2023; plumbers have an unemployment rate of 15.1%.

168.   The lifespan of a brand new washing machine is 11 years.

169.   Petrichor is the technical term for the smell of rain.

170.   The Sarajevo Sahat Tower in Bosnia & Herzegovina is a historic

timepiece which said to be is the only clock in the world that keeps lunar time.

171. The 2002 Grand National was won by Bindaree, it had initial odds of winning the race of 20 to 1.

172. Chestnut is a very common coat colour for horses, the wide range of shades can cause confusion as the lightest chestnuts may be mistaken for palominos, while the darkest shades can be so dark they appear black.

173. In 1498, the bristle toothbrush was invented in China; the bristles were made from coarse hairs taken from the back of a hog's neck and attached to handles made of bone or bamboo.

174. According to a 2022 study by Complete Sports, Arsenal fans were found to be the least intelligent.

175. In the same survey, Liverpool fans were found to be the most annoying on social media.

176. 2 litres is just over 405 U.S. teaspoons.

177. "He's got a brand new car, looks like a jaguar" are the opening words to the Feeder song "Buck Rogers".

178. In 1999, Paris was Europe's most visited city.

179. On Rue Saint-Denis in Paris, there is a Haitian restaurant called Riz Djondjon with an average rating of 4.3 stars on Google as of May 2023.

180. The world's largest paper cup sculpture is situated in Riverside, California; it stands 68 feet high.

181. In the 2001 UK census, the population of Oldham, Greater Manchester; was 103,544.

182. The book "Almost Black" by Vijay Jojo Chokal-Ingam was published on 13th September 2016 and has 352 pages.

183. An Ipsos survey conducted in 2021 discovered that 22% of Americans' favourite type of doughnut was cream-filled.

184. A YouGov survey found that in 2022, 39% of Brits preferred Raspberry Jam doughnuts.

185. In the same survey, plain Custard was the nation's 3rd most popular doughnut, preferred by 21% of respondents.

186. In the city of Wuppertal, Germany; there is a bridge that is painted in the style of Lego bricks, it is known as the "Lego Bridge".

187. Harry and Esther Snyder who founded the In-N-Out fast food chain, pioneered the very first 'drive-thru' service in 1948.

188. The Ford Fiesta is a supermini hatchback sold by the Ford Motor

Company predominantly in Europe since its production in 1976.

189. As of the 17th May 2023, Jack Soley's book "500 Useless Facts That Nobody Wanted To Know" sold 84 units.

190. The most expensive Warhammer 40,000 model sold at auction was an all-metal Thunderhawk Gunship produced in 1997 by Games Workshop, it sold for $34,882.

191. According to the World Bank in 2021, the unemployment rate of Afghanistan was 13.30%.

192. Archduke Franz Ferdinand was elevated to the military rank of a lieutenant at age fourteen.

193. Scottish rock band Franz Ferdinand's lead singer Alex Kapranos, was awarded the "Alumnus of the Year" award by Stratchclyde University in 2005.

194. Sunderland AFC was promoted to the First Division of English football in 1990 after play-off winners Swindon Town were disqualified after being guilty of breaching financial conduct rules relating to illegal payments.

195. There are around 200 calories in a pint of Guinness.

196. As of 2016, only 2% of the population of the Republic of Ireland speak Irish as their first language.

197. In 2022, a Greek woman was given a parking ticket that totalled €6,648,444 and even though this was the result of a clerical error, this is still thought to be the most expensive parking ticket issued.

198. In the state of Iowa, you are not allowed to charge for your piano performance if you only have one arm.

199. A shark's age can be identified by counting the rings on their vertebrae.

200. "The Coronation of Edward VII" is a short silent film directed by Georges Méliès in 1902, it's a staged simulation of the actual coronation that took place during that year of the new king & queen; it has a run time of approximately 6 minutes.

201. In 2007, Starbucks and Concord Music Group launched the Hear Music record label, the label's first signing was Paul McCartney.

202. "The Year of Living Dangerously" starring Sigourney Weaver and Mel Gibson was set in Indonesia.

203. The 'Toy of the Year' awarded by the Toy Retailers Association is awarded to the most innovative, creative, and diverse toy that exists within the industry year on year, in 2004 it was awarded to the RoboSapien.

204. The remote control for the RoboSapien toy has 21 buttons and with

2 shift buttons, the toy has a total of 67 executable commands.

205. In Singapore, all male citizens and permanent residents with some exceptions are required to carry out a period of National Service.

206. For many years in the UK, refuse skips had to be painted yellow as studies shown that yellow was the most visible colour in the dark; however a lot of skips nowadays have reflective stickers and lights on them so the requirement that a skip needed to be yellow has been dropped.

207. The first item ever sold on eBay was a broken laser pointer, it was sold by founder Pierre Omidyar and bought by Mark Fraser.

208. When "Jerry Springer: The Opera" aired on British television in January 2005, the broadcaster BBC Two received 55,000 complaints from viewers.

209. "Jerry Springer: The Opera" was the winner of the 2004 Laurence Olivier award for Best New Musical.

210. A salt dosage of 1 to 3 grams per kilogram of body weight is lethal. If you weighed 85 kilograms, 255 grams of salt would be more than enough to kill you.

211. Google Doodle's have never been dedicated to people who are still alive.

212. The Apple iPhone 12 has a battery capacity of 2,815 mAh.

213. When measuring tyres, the two digit number after the forward slash means the aspect ratio, If a tyre is "205/65 R14" the 65 means that the height is equal to 65% of the tyre's width.

214. The exact origin of the phrase "make like a tree and leave" is lost to history but the phrase was most well known after the 1980s movie "Back to the Future".

215. The collective noun for moles is a 'labour' or a 'company'.

216. Using just the letters, 'Christmas' scores 16 points in Scrabble.

217. The boiling point of Xenon is -108 degrees centigrade.

218. The inventor of the vertical file cabinet is disputed between Henry Brown, Edwin Seibels, Nathaniel Rosenau, and David E. Hunter; most reputable sources have determined that Seibels was the man responsible for the invention.

219. The volume of Lake Balaton in Hungary is the equivalent of 6,687,000,000,000 imperial cups.

220. The name of the country of Panama is translated into Russian as "village of fishermen".

221. U.S. President Lyndon B. Johnson granted 364 presidential pardons in the year 1966.

222. The foundations for Lincoln Cathedral were laid in 1072 and were consecrated in 1092.

223. In 1939, there was 439,694 marriages in England and Wales.

224. It used to be illegal to change a light bulb in Victoria, Australia; the only people who were allowed to change bulbs were certified electricians.

225. The starting price for the Dell Latitude E6430 when it was introduced in 2012 was $749.

226. The ISO 3166 or Alpha 2 country code for Algeria is DZ.

227. The most stable isotope of Bohrium has a half life of just under 2 and a half minutes.

228. Between 2010 and 2022, some Belling, Stoves, and New World gas range cookers manufactured by Glen Dimplex were recalled due to a risk of carbon monoxide poisoning when the grill door was closed.

229. Count Isamu Yoshii was a Japanese poet and playwright who died at the age of 74.

230. In 2021, China was the world's largest producer of Silk.

231. If a bird is preening, it is cleaning its feathers.

232. Born in 1779, William Hedley gave the name "Puffing Billy" to his early railway locomotive.

233. Emil Jannings was the first male winner of an Oscar and as of 2023 is the only German to have won the Academy Award for Best Actor.

234. The height difference between the vaulting horses used in men and women's gymnastics is 15 centimetres.

235. Woman's Hour first broadcast in the year 1946, is now a regular slot on BBC Radio 4 in the UK.

236. Frank Baker the baseball player, was given the nickname "Home Run".

237. In Egypt, Ankhkare was a pharaoh that ruled in the 14th dynasty.

238. Italian football club Juventus was founded in the year 1897.

239. Jan Kincaid, drummer for the band Brand New Heavies was also in the band K Collective.

240. Slaughterhouse-Five published by Kurt Vonnegut in 1969 has 190 pages in its first edition and features a character called Billy Pilgrim.

241. John Cleese played nearly-headless Nick in Harry Potter and the Philosopher's Stone.

242. Mediolanum was the Roman name for the city of Milan.

243. The island of Guernsey was known to the Romans as Sarnia.

244. In British Greyhound racing, the Number 1 dog wears a red jacket.

245. In British Greyhound racing, the Number 2 dog wears a blue jacket.

246. The first auto-pilot system for aeroplanes was developed by the Sperry Corporation in 1912.

247. Egg whites is the primary ingredient of Royal icing.

248. The Cassia spice, also known as Chinese cinnamon is obtained from the bark of the Cinnamomum aromaticum tree.

249. To celebrate 10 years of 'The Simpsons', the British magazine Radio Times issued 4 different exclusive covers to mark the milestone; one with Marge and Maggie together, Homer, Lisa, and Bart Simpson.

250. "Moaning Lisa" was the very first episode of The Simpsons to be censored by the BBC; this was due to a video game in the episode that Homer and Bart were playing being a little too violent.

251. The film 'Becket' was nominated for 12 Oscars but only won one.

252. According to historical records, the London district of Ham was first recorded in 1086, this area became what we now know today as West Ham.

253. "I'm Forever Blowing Bubbles" is a popular American song written in 1918 that is now the anthem of the Premier League football club, West Ham.

254. Jean-Pierre Fux is a world champion in Body Building.

255. 21 degrees Fahrenheit is -6.1 degrees centigrade.

256. "The Exchange" is a play and novel published by Yuri Trifonov in 1969.

257. The modern 26th wedding anniversary gift is Pictures.

258. The modern 27th wedding anniversary gift is Sculptures.

259. The traditional 8th wedding anniversary gift is bronze in the U.S. and salt in the UK.

260. The first jet-powered helicopter to be mass produced was the SNCASO SO 1221 Djinn; it had a maximum speed of 81 mph.

261. On the 15th October 1996, a double decker bus deliberately drove into Whitehouse Bridge in Swindon as a planned stunt to warn transport companies of the dangers that bridges can inflict; the bridge often features in the list of most hit bridges in the UK.

262. The Google Pixel 7A was released in May 2023, it has a 4,385 mAh battery and had an introductory price of £449 in the UK.

263.   The Apocalypse was a ride at Drayton Manor Theme Park that opened on the 27th May 2000 and was closed on the 30th October 2022; its operating speed was 50mph.

264.   The Parotid is the name of the human body's main saliva gland.

265.   1974 was the year in which the first programmable pocket calculator was invented.

266.   "For Your Eyes Only" was a James Bond film starring Roger Moore and featured Britain's Polaris Submarines.

267.   Indolence is an alternative word for Laziness.

268.   "Act Naturally" is a track found on the Beatles' album "Help!"

269.   Cheese is the primary ingredient in Mornay sauce.

270.   In the film "Gattaca", the 2 brothers competed in a swimming race.

271. Bronze is an alloy of Tin and Copper.

272. The Credit card was first invented in 1950 by Frank McNamara and Ralph Schneider.

273. The word 'Grandfather' in Scrabble is worth 19 points.

274. George Blaisdel invented the Zippo lighter in the year 1932.

275. There are 639 named muscles in the human body.

276. In 1934, entrepreneur J.F. Cantrell opened the world's first laundrette initially named a "Washateria" in Fort Worth, Texas.

277. The Schwerer Gustav was a German railway gun that could fire shells weighing 7 tons, each unit cost 7 million Reichsmarks to produce and only 2 were built.

278. The peace symbol incorporates the letters N & D in semaphore, these letters were chosen as they mean 'Nuclear Disarmament'.

279. The national anthems of Liechtenstein and Great Britain share the same melody.

280. Mosquitoes and their larvae will die at around 50 degrees Fahrenheit.

281. Only female mosquitoes bite.

282. Bonzi Buddy is a computer program now described as adware and spyware that was originally released in 1999 by Joe and Jay Bonzi.

283. When a lightning bolt strikes earth, it's around 5 times hotter than the surface of the sun.

284. Ghana means 'Warrior King' in Mande, a language spoken in West Africa.

285. As of January 1ˢᵗ 2023, all works published in the United States before January 1ˢᵗ 1928 are in the public domain.

286. The oldest recognisable recording of a human voice was an excerpt from the song "Au clair de la lune" recorded in 1860.

287. Gypsum plaster also known as 'Plaster of Paris' was given its name because it was originally made by heating gypsum from a deposit in Montmatre, a hill in Paris.

288. "Commedia dell'arte" literally meaning comedy of the profession, originated from Italian theatre that was popular in Europe between the 16ᵗʰ and 18ᵗʰ centuries; in terms of their social class and religion, actors were known for their diversity and would perform anywhere they could.

289. The most expensive whiskey ever sold at auction was on Saint Patrick's Day in 2021 when the Craft Irish

Whiskey Company in partnership with Fabergé, sold its Emerald Isle Collection for $2 million.

290.   The word cnidarian comes from the Greek for "sea nettle" which includes sea anemone, corals, and jellyfish.

291.   Johnny Depp's first film role was of Glen Lantz in "Nightmare on Elm Street".

292.   The Lodge is the primary residence of the Prime Minister of Australia, it's located at 5 Adelaide Avenue in Canberra.

293.   Anathema is another word for excommunication.

294.   A last is a tool used by a cobbler or shoemaker that resembles a human foot.

295.   An arctophile is someone who collects teddy bears.

296. In the UK, if you watch live television you need to buy a television licence which as of 2023, costs £159 for a colour TV licence or £53.50 for a black and white (monochrome) TV licence.

297. As of 31st March 2022, there were just over 4,000 monochrome TV licences in force in the UK.

298. The Ashes is a series that consists of five Cricket tests, competed by England and Australia at least once every two years. The Ashes are regarded as being held by the team that most recently won the series. If the series is drawn, the team that currently holds the Ashes retains the trophy.

299. The urn awarded to the winner of The Ashes, is long believed to contain the cremated ashes of a cricket bail or the remains of a lady's veil.

300. 'Garash' is a chocolate cake containing walnuts, egg whites, and sugar that's a popular dish in Bulgarian cuisine despite it being invented by the Austro-Hungarian confectioner, Kosta Garash.

301. Because of its wet surface and cloud humidity, there is a possibility that rainbows may exist on Saturn's moon, Titan.

302. From the 1st April 2021, if you want to add a name or change the name of your house in the borough of West Devon, it'll cost you £25 per property.

303. In 1932, first sunscreen was invented in Australia by the chemist Milton Blake.

304. In 1936, L'Oréal released its first sunscreen product.

305. L'Oréal was founded by Frenchman Eugène Schueller.

306. On the 9th February 1893, the opera "Falstaff" by Giuseppe Verdi premièred at La Scala in Milan.

307. In flooring, Scotia the name given to the decorative shaping used to cover a gap between the ground and the baseboard running along the bottom of a wall.

308. An eggcorn is a word or phrase that's often used by mistake, a common example is "doggy-dog world" instead of the correct, "dog-eat-dog world".

309. Coming from the German to mean a compulsion to move, Zugzwang is a situation found in Chess and other turn based games where a player is forced to make a move that would disadvantage their current position.

310. Long Life Milk is rapidly heated then packaged in a way that's free from all contamination, the heat is intended to reduce bacteria giving the milk an extended shelf life.

311. According to the BBC, in 2022 one phone was stolen every 6 minutes in

London, only 2% of stolen phones are recovered.

312. The average human produces around 500 grams of excrement per day.

313. Half a cup of bogeys or boogers, contain 25 calories.

314. The word 'key' is masculine in German but feminine in Spanish.

315. The longest arm hair ever recorded was just under 22cm and was on the arm of American David Reed.

316. "Viva La Vida" by Coldplay doesn't mention the title of the song in its lyrics.

317. Pine needles can be brewed into a tea that can fight off scurvy.

318. Scurvy is the disease caused by a lack of Vitamin C in the diet, there were 171 cases of the disease in England during 2020-21.

319. Woodstock '99 was a music festival that took place in Rome, New York from July 22nd to July 25th 1999.

320. The prize for winning a game in Downtown London Pub in Miniclip's 8 Ball Pool, is 100 coins.

321. The price for a litre of standard unleaded at the Shell Tothill Services near the A34 in Hampshire at 6pm on the 23rd June 2023, was £1.499 per litre.

322. The price for a Venti Mocha at the Starbucks at Tothill Services on the 23rd June 2023, was £5.15.

323. In 2018, a puppet from the British children's TV series Sooty dating from the 1950s, sold at auction for £14,500.

324. According to a 2018 report, Fibromyalgia occurs in all populations across the world and is a condition that can affect all ages, the condition affects somewhere between 2-3% of the global population. Women are more likely to experience Fibromyalgia than men.

325. It is estimated that there are 110 million land mines in the ground, an equal amount is present in stockpiles.

326. If you're playing a game of Minesweeper and you uncover an 8, that means that every square surrounding it horizontally, vertically, and diagonally, is a mine and should be avoided.

327. The nearest land to the Antipodal point of Mecca, is Tematangi Island in French Polynesia.

328. The Church of God of Prophecy is a Pentecostal branch of the Christian faith, it was one of five Church of God bodies that arose from a gathering near the Tennessee and North Carolina border on 13th June 1903.

329. Wouter André De Backer is the birth name of the Belgian born, Australian singer-songwriter, Gotye.

330. Paraguay uses the Type C plug sockets, the standard voltage of its electricity is 220 volts with a frequency of 50Hz.

331. The company ADT provides 80% of alarm services in the United States.

332. According to Real Homes, the household appliance most likely to catch fire is the Cooker.

333. In the same study, the 6th appliance most likely to catch fire was the washing machine.

334. F is the failing grade in the U.S. letter grading system used in schools.

335. In the same grading system, D is a passing grade and is usually awarded for scores between 59-69%.

336. Research conducted by Zoopla, found that houses at Number 1 are on average, the most expensive.

337. The average annual salary for a 25-34 year old in Canada is CAD $46,900.

338. Noah "Puck" Puckerman is a character from the TV series Glee, he was played by Mark Salling who died on January 30, 2018.

339. "Ekstraklasa" is the name of the top tier of Polish football, the 2022/23 season was won by Raków Częstochowa, winning the league for the first time in their history.

340. "Where did I go wrong I lost a friend, somewhere along in the bitterness, and I would have stayed up with you all night had I known how to save a life" is the chorus in The Fray's 2006 song "How To Save A Life".

341. The Grace Line passenger and cargo ocean liner 'SS Santa Lucia' was also known as the 'USS Leedstown (AP-73)' the ship was acquired by the U.S. Navy in August 1942 and was sunk off the coast of Algeria in November 1942.

342. Born on the 28th February 1942, Rolling Stones member Brian Jones was also known as "Elmo Lewis" during a brief spell as a Blues musician.

343. Smooth jazz saxophonist George Howard released his first 4 albums on the 'Palo Alto' record label; he died on the 20th March 1998, my birthday.

344. The logo of British Petroleum is known as the 'Helios' and it is a white, yellow, and green star with 18 points.

345. In the UK, it is not illegal to eat while behind the wheel of a vehicle.

346. Medication containing Pseudoephedrine commonly found in vapour rubs are not allowed in Japan.

347. "Sailing By" is a short piece of light music composed by Ronald Binge in 1963, which is used before the Shipping Forecast on BBC Radio 4 which is usually broadcast 12 minutes before 1am.

348. The 21st prime number is 73.

349. The most common size for clay bricks used in the UK, is 215mm x 102.5mm x 65mm.

350. The word 'Sandcastle' contains 3 syllables.

351. Grégoire Akcelrod is a former French footballer who claimed to play for the Ligue 1 club Paris Saint-Germain, he almost signed for Bulgarian team CSKA Sofia, however the transfer was cancelled when the ruse was exposed and that he never played for the first team of the club.

352. In 2005, the website MySpace was sold to News Corp for $580 million.

353. Eton College is a public school founded by King Henry VI in 1440.

354. A survey conducted in 2022, discovered that the most popular Halloween candy for Americans' is Reese's Cups, 2nd is Skittles, 3rd is M&Ms.

355. A new poll published in 2023, claimed that 'technical difficulties' are among the most common excuses for not working by remote workers.

356. According to the Organisation of Autism Research, around 1 in 68 people have some form of autism.

357. "I hate my current job" according to the Australian website Outplacement, is the worst thing to say in a job interview.

358. Mary Anderson invented the windscreen wiper in 1902, she didn't drive.

359. For the first time ever in 2022, New Zealand did not record a single death relating to AIDS for an entire year.

360. Plaxton is an English builder of bus and coach bodies, the company has its headquarters in Eastfield, near Scarborough.

361. It takes light 1.33 seconds for light to reach the earth from the Moon.

362. The most common phobia in India, is Glossophobia; the fear of public speaking.

363. In India, agricultural income from land situated in India is exempted from taxation.

364. U.S. Route 59 has a length of 1,911 miles (3,075 kilometres) and passes through Texas, Arkansas, Oklahoma, Kansas, Missouri, Iowa, and Minnesota.

365. The Dukedom of Tamames is a hereditary title in the Spanish peerage;

it is currently vacant and was created by King Charles IV of Spain.

366. After a Netflix adaptation of "13 Reasons Why", the 2007 book of the same name is now one of the most restricted books in American schools and colleges due to its themes regarding suicide, drug use, and sex.

367. BBC Red Button is an interactive television brand used in the United Kingdom, it was founded in 1999 and encourages viewers to press the red button on their TV remote to access other services on their receiver, such as news, weather, and other hidden features.

368. When the Titanic sank, White Star Line stopped the pay of the crew at the moment of the sinking, but later charged families the freight costs of shipping the bodies back.

369. After the Titanic sank, the families of the band members who died were billed by White Star Line for the cost of their uniforms.

370. The founders of the restaurant chain Outback Steakhouse intentionally decided not to visit Australia, as they had worries that having too much authenticity would confuse and potentially scare away customers.

371. American singer and ukulele player Tiny Tim married the then 17-year-old Victoria Budinger at the age of 37; the marriage was broadcast on The Tonight Show Starring Johnny Carson on 17th December 1969.

372. It takes light 8 minutes and 20 seconds to reach the earth from the sun, 2 seconds longer than the pilot episode of Spongebob Squarepants.

373. This font is called Bahnschrift.

374. The mean BMI for men in the Netherlands according to a World

Health Organisation study in 2015, was 25.9.

375. "Porch Pirate" was added to the Oxford English Dictionary in 2023, the official definition is: "a person who steals parcels that have been delivered and left unattended outside the intended recipient's home, business, etc..."

376. The world's oldest terrarium is claimed to be in possession of Englishman David Latimer, he planted a single tradescantia cutting in 1960 and was last opened in 1972.

377. Every year, the U.S. government tries to pay Cuba for leasing the land of Guantanamo Bay; since the revolution of 1959, only one payment was cashed.

378. In 1998, a Pixar employee accidentally deleted Toy Story 2 from their system and all the files were removed; luckily, an employee who had been working from home had a backup copy on her computer, the backup was found and recovered therefore saving the film; however, bosses didn't think the movie was good enough and it was mostly remade.

379. A nesiote person would most likely live on an island.

380. Judas Priest took their name from the Bob Dylan song "The Ballad of Frankie Lee and Judas Priest".

381. Jan Baptist van Helmont coined the term 'gas' from the Greek word 'chaos'.

382. The inside diameter of the net ring in basketball is 18 inches.

383. Wisdom teeth also known as third molars are the last teeth to come in at the back of each side of the jaw.

384. In Italy, there is no jury in civil proceedings.

385. In Belgium, any citizen aged between 28 and 65 may be called upon to undertake jury service.

386. In 1994, a murder case in the UK had to be re-tried because some members of the jury tried to contact the murdered victim through a Ouija board in their hotel, the judge found out and dismissed the jury, but had this happened in the jury room, the judge couldn't have dismissed them.

387. In 2021, British police recorded 58 cases of Bigamy.

388. In Leonardo Da Vinci's 'The Last Supper', the apostles on Jesus' left in order of left to right are: Thomas, James Major, Philip, Matthew, Thaddeus, and Simon.

389. A baldric is a belt worn over a shoulder that is typically used to carry a sword.

390. Baldrick is the name of several fictional characters in the BBC television series Blackadder, the character is portrayed in all series by Tony Robinson.

391. Allspice is the name given to the dried, unripe fruits of the pimento tree.

392. In Greek mythology, the tale of Pandora's Box begins with Zeus and other gods creating Pandora, the first human woman.

393. Simnel cake is a fruitcake most associated with Easter and Lent.

394. In the TV series 24, Jack Bauer's daughter is named Kim.

395. Anserine is an adjective that relates to Geese.

396. Anserine is a dipeptide containing Beta-alanine and 3-methylhistidine, it can be found in the skeletal muscle and brain of mammals and birds.

397. The UNESCO World Heritage Site of Jam is situated in Ghor Province, Afghanistan.

398. Evangelista Torricelli was a student of Galileo Galilei, he is best known for inventing the barometer.

399. The coldest temperature ever recorded in Shenzhen, China was 0.2 degrees centigrade on the 11th February 1957.

400. "Winnipeg" or "Winnie" was the name given to a female black bear that lived in London Zoo from 1915 until her death in 1934; the bear was the inspiration for the A.A. Milne Winnie-the-Pooh books, and was a regimental mascot for the Canadian Army Veterinary Corps.

401. Hedy Lamarr was an actress and inventor who co-patented a secret communication system with her husband in the early 1940's, the technology in this patent is now used in

Bluetooth, GPS, and earlier versions of modern Wi-Fi.

402. There is a misconception that Wi-Fi is the abbreviation for "Wireless Fidelity", it was actually unintentionally created by the Wi-Fi Alliance itself when Wi-Fi was introduced during the late 1990s.

403. In International paper sizes, the A series of paper sizes is used for books, magazines, and writing; the C series was predominantly used for envelopes.

404. The first documented case of a 404 error message appearing on a web page; was in 1993, when a user tried to access a page about the Mosaic web browser. The page had been moved to a different location, but the link had not been updated.

405. The Peugeot 405 was voted European Car of the Year in 1988.

406. King George III was the last English sovereign at his coronation to claim to be King of France.

407. Henri Rousseau was a French impressionist painter who was nicknamed "Le Douanier" because of his past occupation as a customs official.

408. The only integer that's neither positive nor negative is 0.

409. In Norse mythology, Sleipnir is the name of Odin's 8 legged horse who could travel across land, air, and sea.

410. Amarula is a cream liqueur from South Africa, it is made from sugar, cream, and the fruit of the marula or Sclerocarya birrea tree.

411. When referring to cutlery, the points or the teeth on a fork are called tines.

412. Zinc pyrithione is a compound that has a melting point of 240 degrees centigrade, it is known for its antibacterial properties and most well known for treating dandruff.

413. Pediculus humanus capitis is the trinomial name for the head louse, adult lice can live up to 30 days on a human head.

414. A raw apricot contains around 17 calories.

415. The most stolen item from supermarkets according to a UK based survey in 2022, was packed meat.

416. The second most stolen item in the same survey, was razor blades.

417. In the U.S. state of Ohio, it is illegal to kill a housefly within 160 feet of a church without a license.

418. 'Shinygite' is an anagram of Hygienist.

419. "Down to Earth: The Life and Views of Ted Moult" is a 1973 autobiography that consists of 224 pages.

420. Pelly Ruddock Mpanzu is the first footballer to make it from the non-league tiers of English football to the Premier League with the same club, having played for Luton Town since 2013.

421. The year 1949 in the Japanese calendar is Shōwa 24.

422. The Sukhoi Su-17 is a fighter bomber produced by the Soviet Union between 1967-1990, a total 2,867 aircraft were built.

423. In some parts of the East end of London, you can find cash machines that'll give you "Cockney Rhyming Slang" as a language option; you can choose to withdraw 'Sausage & Mash' (Cash) or even change your 'Huckleberry Finn' (pin).

424. The most common age range for a divorce in the UK in 2022, was 40-44.

425. House fly eggs take between 8 and 24 hours to hatch.

426. Exoneration refers to being cleared of a crime due to new evidence of your innocence, and the condemned has the civil status they had prior to their conviction.

427. Pardoning is a form of clemency that forgives a condemned person for a crime that was committed.

428. In 2003, the Italian-Dutch space observatory 'BeppoSAX' crashed in the Pacific Ocean.

429. There are wristwatches you can buy that will run on Martian Time, as a day on Mars is just short of 24 hours and 40 minutes.

430. Actor Richard E. Grant is a dual citizen of the United Kingdom and Eswatini, he used to wear a watch on each wrist; one of them was permanently set to Liswati time.

431. Eswatini was formerly known as Swaziland before the country officially renamed itself on 19th April 2018.

432. A radio button is a control on a computer that allows the user to choose only one option out of a multiple choice, when a new selection is chosen the other previously chosen option is de-selected.

433. Emtel Ltd is a communications company based in Mauritius; it claims to be the first mobile telephony operator in the Southern Hemisphere.

434. William Kamkwamba is a Malawian inventor who gained notoriety when he built a wind turbine to power electrical appliances in his family's house, a solar powered water pump that supplied the first drinking water in his village; he was unable to continue education due to growing up in relative poverty but after an invitation to a conference in Tanzania, investors funded his secondary education.

435. Most people wear their watches on their non-dominant hand, so left-handed people would typically wear a watch on their right hand.

436. Horatio Nelson lost his right arm and right eye in battle.

437. HMS Warrior was put up for sale as scrap in 1924, after there were no buyers; the ship left Portsmouth in 1929 and was converted into an oil jetty.

438. The keychain fastener used to prevent burglaries, was patented by Frederick J. Loudin in 1894.

439. At the end of the 4th quarter of 2022, the Ford Focus had 1,295 models in the colour Purple registered on British roads.

440. Dubbed the 'ugliest colour in the world' Pantone 448 C is described as a drab and dark brown.

441. A study of American schoolchildren found that in 2012, the most hated colour was Orange.

442. The name of the phobia relating to the colour Orange or the fruit of the same name, is arantiophobia.

443. A 2016 article revealed that the worst thing that a patient can do to their doctor is to be untruthful.

444. In the same article, patients complaining about other doctors was 4th.

445. St. James's Park station on the London Underground has changed its name 3 times, tube maps up to the early 1930s show the name as "St. James' Park"; In 1933 until the early 1950s, the name was shown as "St. James Park". Since the 1950s it has been known by it's current name.

446. "Don't You Know Who I Think I Am?" is a 200 page book written by Justin Ross Lee in 2016.

447. "Olykoek" is an alternative name for a doughnut, this name originally comes from the Dutch for 'oily cake'.

448. If the cables snapped and brakes failed in an elevator, the elevator would fall upwards as the counterweight that supports the weight of the cab is heavier than the cab itself.

449. Most wasabi is often served in shops and restaurants is ordinary horseradish, this is because wasabi is more expensive and as a cost saving measure, horseradish is dyed green to give the impression of tucking into wasabi.

450. Chinese Porcelain is often referred to by its shorter name, China.

451. In 2019, the European Union's biggest exporter of watches and clocks was France.

452. The International Peace Garden is a garden that straddles the border between Canada and the United States in Manitoba and North Dakota respectively, visitors from either country can enter the park via their national highways and can cross the international boundary without restrictions, but the border controls are just outside of the garden area.

453. Coca-Cola was the first soft drink to be consumed in space on 12th July 1985.

454. Mário Ferreira became the first Portuguese person to travel to space in 2022.

455. Sara Sabry was the first Egyptian, first Arab woman, and first African woman to travel into space on the same space mission.

456. The world's first modern air conditioning system was invented by Willis Carrier in 1902, initially to solve high humidity in a printing shop.

457. On the Beaufort scale, a gale is signified by the number 8.

458. In the TV series "Absolutely Fabulous", Patsy's surname is Stone.

459. Towa Tei, DJ Krush, and Cornelius are all musical icons from Japan.

460. An irascible person is susceptible to anger.

461. François Delecour is a French rally car driver.

462. The bass line in "I Got The..." by Labi Siffre was sampled in the Eminem song "My Name Is".

463. Albedo is a measure to determine how reflective a surface is on a scale from 0 to 1, the more reflective a surface is, the higher its albedo number.

464. "Don't push me, 'cause I'm close to the edge" are words often featured in the Grandmaster Flash song "The Message".

465. Niaiserie is a word meaning to be simple or foolish.

466. In 1994, Colombia produced more coal than France.

467. Pago Pago is the capital of the territory of American Samoa.

468. The official currency of Guatemala is the Quetzal.

469. Ancient Greeks and Ancient Romans were known to have used cobwebs to stop bleeding.

470. The first Christmas Day message by a British monarch was in 1932, when King George V broadcast live to the empire from Sandringham House.

471. The first product advertised on British television, was toothpaste.

472. London was the first city to host the Olympic Games three times in 1908, 1948, and 2012.

473. In the Pentagon, there are a total of 284 restrooms; this was because when the Pentagon was being built, it had to comply with Virginia's racial segregation laws that existed during the time.

474. "In God We Trust" is the official motto of the United States found on its currency; however, "E pluribus unum" has also been used as a motto found on the Great Seal of the United States.

475. In some languages, the letter 'W' is a vowel, not a consonant.

476. Burnished Brass is a moth that feed on the flowers of the Honeysuckle plant.

477. Infants normally have around 30,000 tastebuds compared to around 10,000 for an adult.

478. Gypsy Creams are an oat biscuit with a buttercream filling.

479. 2007 was the Year of the Pig in the Chinese zodiac.

480. In the western zodiac; Cancer, Scorpio, and Pisces are water signs.

481. Kuopion Palloseura, also known as KuPS, is a football club from Finland that has won the top flight of Finnish football six times as of June 2023.

482. In a lifetime, an average person will grow 590 miles of hair.

483. Nails will grow faster in the summer than the winter.

484. Most kites will fly well in breezes of up to 9 knots.

485. The global average age for a person having their first child in 2023, is 28 years old.

486. The most dispensed prescription drug in England in 2020-21 was Atorvastatin, it is used to treat high blood cholesterol.

487. LASER stands for Light Amplification by Stimulated Emission of Radiation.

488. MASER is the same system as a LASER but instead of amplifying light, a MASER amplifies microwaves.

489. According to a 2023 study, 55% of internet users across the world preferred Ranch sauce to BBQ sauce.

490. Sororal is an adjective that means sisterly.

491. Dendrochronology is the science of dating tree rings.

492. Punto Banco is a variety of the casino game Baccarat.

493. "The homestead of the people of Snot" is the literal Saxon meaning of the city of Nottingham.

494. You can produce just under 2 litres of mucus every day.

495. Your dominant nostril changes up to once every 3 hours.

496. William Shakespeare became a shareholder in the Globe Theatre, paying £10 for his 12.5% share.

497. The murder of Abel by Cain is told in the Genesis book of the Bible.

498. "I needed a drink, I needed a lot of life insurance, I needed a vacation, I needed a home in the country. What I had was a coat, a hat, and a gun." is a quote by character Philip Marlowe in the 1940 novel "Farewell, My Lovely".

499. Texas landowner, Jimmie Luecke has the world's largest signature on his land; his surname is spelled out across three miles of trees.

500. Dalmatian Jasper is a stone that is said to help find forgiveness and make relationships more enjoyable, this stone is predominantly mined in Chihuahua, Mexico.

www.ingramcontent.com/pod-product-compliance
Lightning Source LLC
Chambersburg PA
CBHW011421070526
44584CB00026BA/3789